BYRON COMEDY TOUR

ISBN: 9798690101190

Cover photo taken at *Way Out West*, a cool antique store located at: 11610 W White Road, Spokane, WA.

MATTBYRON.COM

BYRON COMEDY TOUR

FIRST EDITION

MATT BYRON

CONTENTS

ACKNOWLEDGMENT

I want to thank Lauren DiGiovani for her tremendous support.

Airports & Airplanes

- Airlines charge extra fees for the wrong things. Rather than charging fifty dollars for an extra bag they should charge me fifty dollars to sit next to a hilarious and brilliant woman. Or they could charge me one hundred dollars so I don't have to sit near crying babies or people who smell gross.

- Do airplane pilots get speeding tickets? Or do they get speeding bonuses?

- When customers board the airplane they should announce that the captain is getting over a bitter divorce and drug addiction. Then the airline could sell life insurance to customers.

- Why bother with the airplane seatbelt? When was the last time you ever heard of an airplane crash where passengers who wore their seatbelts survived? Let's not sugar coat it. If the plane goes down, we're all going to die. Keep us scared. Be honest.

- Why do they start the flights by telling me the most insignificant details? The captain will say we're traveling at 40,000 feet, burning two tons of fuel per hour and the plane was built in 2020.

If I wanted to know all the details, I would fly the plane. Is the captain asking for my opinion? Should I interrupt and say, "You should fly at 32,107 feet today."

- It seems like every plane has a crackly audio system. Why do cars that cost only twenty thousand dollars have better sound systems than one hundred million dollar airplanes?

- Have you ever seen people on an airplane sit in the wrong seat? How hard is it to read a seat number?

- If you find yourself bored at the airport, keep count of how many people smile as they walk by. I've found that depending on the region of the United States, the smile count varies widely.

- Why does airport security ask if I have liquids or dangerous objects in my bag? Are all liquids dangerous? Do they really expect terrorists to tell the truth?

- True story: Airport security literally confiscated my inert bottled water, while an elderly woman with an oxygen tank was invited to bypass the body scanning machine.

- I can't help but wonder how many people at the airport have counterfeit purses and counterfeit luggage. If these ladies really did spend five thousand dollars on their purses, then why are they flying coach?

- Why are the people in first class so smug? They roll their eyes or often avoid eye contact while I walk back to coach. I should be consoling them for being so insecure.

- When I use the restroom on an airplane I feel like I'm coordinating a heist. There's always the "lookout" - where I spin my head around and eye the restroom. Then when nobody is there, I make a run for it. I tap the guy on my left and motion that I need to step out. I lip sync the word "bathroom." Then he taps the shoulder of the lady to his left. She nods and I make my escape. Ample hand signals are key.

- When I fall asleep on the plane, I'm always worried about being robbed or having my money drop out of my pockets. I wish they made jackets with combination locks on the pockets.

- The armrest on the airplane is a valuable piece of real estate. As a rule, each person gets exclusive use of just one arm rest.

- Where do airlines get the ideas for these flight magazines? They always sell the most bizarre things like nose hair trimmers or fake rocks for hiding keys.

- I'm convinced aeronautical engineers are fools because the digital map in front of my seat is not to scale. The airplane is not the size of Connecticut.

- When boarding the airplane there's always one guy or gal holding up eighty-two people in line. It's like he or she can't decide if the bag should be stored in the overhead bin or on the floor. As if the placement will in any way prevent the bag from getting to the destination? I always give these people my laser eyes, unless he or she is elderly, in which case I smile and help.

- What's up with the word *stow*? I much prefer *store*. Flight attendants often tell people to "stow their luggage..." It drives me nuts. It sounds like a weird accent.

- First class passengers are so eager to get their seats, you might think they had front row seats to a concert.

- Why do people demand to have a drink immediately upon sitting in the airplane? Are they exhausted from rolling their tiny bag down the twenty-two-foot-long corridor?

- Do airplanes have keys or key fobs? I suppose I could search Google to find the answer but that would end my curiosity. Do airplanes have alarms too, so that nobody steals the plane? When the captain locks his or her plane, does he or she click a button and the plane goes, "beep, beep?"

- What happens if the captain loses his or her keys at the bar? Imagine getting ready for your flight and they announce, "Sorry passengers but your captain left her keys at the bar last night, please give us a few minutes as we hot-wire your plane." That would be awkward.

- Do airplanes have a horn, so you can honk at other planes trying to cut you off? Or do they have high beam lights, so you can warn other pilots about speed traps?

- Why do they bother installing those emergency oxygen masks on airplanes - the ones that fall from the ceiling? If my plane is crashing, I don't want to experience the pain from crashing. I'd much rather pass out before impact. I wish they would fill those masks with sleeping gas.

Accents

- Americans love people with accents. Just imagine if Arnold Schwarzeneggeror or Simon Cowell didn't have accents. They would be boring. If you plan to get a job in Hollywood, you'll have a leg up if you were born in a foreign country.

- If you don't have an accent, then move to a foreign country where people think you have one. I once dated a French woman. She told me French women love the American accent. I'm baffled that the American accent is attractive, but I'm not going to argue.

Animals

- Birds are smarter than humans. They fly without GPS, without maps, without jet fuel, and they don't use money. That's brilliant.

- Wild animals have far better health than humans. I've never seen an obese, diabetic wild animal using drugs, drinking or smoking. I never see wild animals in the hospital either.

- In nature all animals are beautiful. Have you ever seen an ugly lion, whale or bird? Of course not. They don't exist. In nature, all animals are beautiful or they die.

Barbecue Grills & BBQs

- For some reason, fires cause us to get philosophical. People love to gather around fires to share their wildest stories and deepest thoughts.

- Normally, burning food is frowned upon. But when you're burning ribs, steaks, burgers, shish kabobs or bacon on the barbecue grill, it's expected. In fact, people love the smell of burning food on the barbecue.

- How is the acronym for barbecue *BBQ*? It's a single word and there's no "Q" in it.

- Summertime barbecuing is perfect for the Fourth of July. This is because nothing screams *Liberty!* quite like an open fire, a propane tank and alcoholic beverages.

- Barbecuing is the ideal cooking method for slobs. It requires no pots, pans or clean up. In fact, it's wise to intentionally leave grease on the grill because it creates a delicious smell. If you're a slob, get a barbecue grill.

Birthdays

- Why is it that teenagers are reckless? If anything, people who are ninety-plus years old should be the most reckless. After all, if you know you're going to die soon, you might as well have a glorious death. When I'm ninety I'll go skydiving and drive Formula 1 race cars.

- Why do we celebrate birthdays? Celebrating the passing of 365 days seems like a completely random life activity. Why not celebrate every ten days, or every one hundred days?

Books

- I get mad when people hoard books. I'm worried we're going to run out of words.

- I've always believed it's hard to control the future, but it's easy to rewrite the past.

- Why must lawyers and college professors stuff their offices with old books? Why can't they share books? Haven't they ever heard of libraries?

- Why do hardcover books come with paper covers? The cover just makes it cumbersome to hold. I usually throw the cover in the trash, but then I feel guilty.

- Reading books is so rare in this day and age. Tell someone you read an entire book and they'll stereotype you as an intellectual.

- I don't care for made-up words like *adulting* and *ginormous*. I don't care if Google recognizes them or not. They're not real.

- I love reading books where the first fifteen pages are the prologue. Then I can skip through fifteen pages, place my bookmark and take a break. It makes me feel like I'm a fast reader.

Boston

- I enjoy taking the subway in Boston known as *The T.* I feel like a VIP when I just wave my monthly subway card to walk on the train. Then I see tourists try to pay with coins and cash and I just shake my head. It's the ultimate tell-tale sign of a tourist.

- The streets of Boston are "designed" like a lobster trap. Once you get in, you'll never get out.

Cars & Trucks

- It's lame when people decorate cars with gun stickers. Why not use the real thing? If you're so tough, put some real gun shots in your truck.

- I wish my car had an LED sign so I could communicate with attractive women when I drive by.

- I enjoy watching people parallel park. Most people crack under the pressure of being watched.

- Why is it that car salesmen tell me not to worry about the total price? Is the car going to be free?

- Rather than paying for a therapist, I recommend going to a car dealership. The salespeople always ask about my personal life, "What do you do for work? How big is your family?" Their attempts to build rapport couldn't be more subtle.

- Why do people get vanity license plates? Do they really want the cops to remember them? If I were a bank robber, I would get the vanity plate *Innocent* or *NotABadGuy*. If I enjoyed speeding I would get the plate *VerySlowDriver*.

- If I have a green light and I yield to a jay walker, am I aiding and abetting a crime?

- SUVs look best when covered in mud. Cars look terrible when covered in mud. If you don't like washing your vehicle, you should get an SUV.

- I get a thrill out of driving down hill with no breaks; I feel like it's free fuel.

- Why is it every time that I go to the auto mechanic, they make it sound like my car was about to blow up? The mechanic always makes me feel so lucky. They're like, "The timing belt of your car was melting the flux capacitor. You're lucky you brought it in when you did. You've got a massive life insurance policy right?"

- Don't you hate going to a crosswalk, pushing the button and holding up the cars? It seems like traffic always clears right before you get the cross walk sign.

- Why are people so protective of their driveways and parking spots? Ever go to someone's house and they tell you where to park? The nerve. I'll do as I please.

- Before buying a car, I like to test the airbags. Unfortunately, most dealers don't like it.

- Being stuck in traffic is great; it gives me time to use dating apps and YouTube.

- Why is it illegal to read text messages while driving? Doesn't driving require that I read road signs?

- The wheel was invented by geniuses, but the tire was invented by idiots. A tire full of air is just like a balloon waiting to pop. I suspect a conspiracy by the Big Tire lobby.

- Hitting other cars shouldn't be so taboo. There's a reason they call them bumpers. They're intended to bump other cars. Why would you ever pay for a feature and not use it?

- It's dangerous to have car insurance. It's an incentive for me to crash my car. I know that with insurance, if I crash my car I get a new one.

- Car seats are so comfortable. Why don't we put them in houses and offices?

- How can people say that driving is dangerous? Yet those same people don't call walking dangerous. When you're walking do you use: turn-signals, lights, a protective metal cage, seatbelt and airbags? Of course not. There is far more safety gear for driving than walking. Walkers have virtually no protection. Therefore walking is more dangerous than driving.

- If it's illegal to drive over one hundred miles per hour, then why is it legal for me to buy a car that drives one hundred miles per hour? Seems like entrapment.

- How is it that people get tired from driving for twelve hours or more? They've been sitting the entire time. It's not like they've run a marathon.

- There is an unspoken rivalry between American-made trucks and Japanese-made cars. Truck drivers hate the fuel-efficient-imported-car drivers.

- True story: The *Check Engine* light of my car came on. So I immediately booked an appointment with my mechanic. After hanging up the phone, the light went off. Rather than calling to cancel the appointment, I crossed my fingers hoping for my car to break down. I hate canceling appointments.

- People who don't use blinkers when driving should be taken off the road.

- People who drive obnoxiously loud vehicles belong in fourth grade.

- Who invented the automobile? The idea sounds rather crazy. They must have thought, "I'll strap myself into a bucket of metal, fill it with gasoline and run a series of explosions. Then I'm going to drive seventy miles per hour head-on towards opposing traffic."

- Car shopping is absolutely exhausting. The sales people always play the *Good Cop, Bad Cop* game where they have to negotiate with the manager "out back." The good cop is your salesman who always goes out back to get you "the deal." The bad cop is always the manager.

- Everyone has a great mechanic. Nobody ever wants to admit they've been using a terrible one.

- Buying a car takes like four hours. Yet the process should take less than four minutes. It's a circus. They always say, "We're selling it below invoice. We just make money on the servicing." Such malarkey…

- When people ask, "What do you drive?", why don't they skip the mystery and ask, "Are you rich? What's your net worth?"

- Isn't it bizarre how people equate owning a nice car to having money? But when you think about it, someone who spends a lot of money on a car has less money to invest in other things. So it's obvious to me that people driving beat-up cars are rich.

- Cars are an easy identifier of political values. Chevy Suburban = Republican. Toyota Prius = Democrat. Cadillac = Mobster. Ford F-150 = Farmer. Minivan = Family.

- If you care about the environment, don't get an electric car with a lead battery. Get a bike or some sandals.

- True story: I once test drove a car and it had so little gas in the tank that I had to refuel during the test drive.

- If a used car is cheap I assume it's stolen. If it's too expensive, I assume it's not stolen. That's why I like to overpay for cars.

- What's wrong with driving with strangers? When I travel by bus, train or plane, I have no idea who's driving.

Childhood

- I miss being a kid and hearing school snow cancelations on the radio. There was so much suspense as I would listen to eighty schools being canceled before hearing mine. But in the modern age kids go online to read cancelations in second. It's just not the same.

- I respect the ambition of fifth graders. They often carry backpacks that are half their body weight.

- Legos satisfy our inner desire to play God. It's hard to replicate the power-trip found in destroying a Lego city.

Cell Phones

- Why must my cell phone constantly update? I just want to call and surf the internet. Has that really changed in twenty years?

- It amazes me how people text on their cell phones while crossing the street. It's as if they want to get hit.

- Have you ever told someone "goodbye" on video chat and then fumbled to click the disconnect button? Awkward…

- When I see people glued to their phones at the train station, I know they're trying to appear important. After all, truly important people travel by plane.

- I love cell phone *Family Plans*. They give families a reason to stick together.

- I dislike wireless cell phone headsets. It makes it hard to tell when people are schizophrenic.

- Why do people send email messages with signature lines like, "Sent from my (insert brand name) phone." That's like spamming friends with banner ads.

- I love using the GPS on my phone for directions. But I find it rude for not saying, "Please" or "Thank you" when I make the correct turn.

- Ever walk into a coffee shop and notice that everyone is absolutely engrossed in their cell phones? These are the same people who just waited twenty minutes in line to order a beverage. They can't possibly be doing anything important.

- Have you seen a cell phone video of a crime taking place? Rather than filming the crime, why didn't the witness call 911?

- Why do concert attendees feel compelled to hold their phones up and film the event? Isn't the very purpose of attending a concert to enjoy it live?

- Cell phone applications are out of control. I do not want to load another app on my phone! I do not want to create another username and password. I do not want to grant another application access to all my personal contacts, emails and pictures. I just want an app that deletes all my apps.

- Have you ever had your cell phone auto-populate your answers? Technology is starting to rule over humans.

- I keep hearing that my cell phone has more computer power than the first space shuttle. So I'd like to know how soon I can buy a space shuttle.

Clothing

- Should I really wear my best shirt on the first date? If my first impression is too good, then things can only decline.

- I don't understand why sweatpants are unacceptable work attire. How does wearing them actually affect the work of an attorney, banker, doctor or anyone else? If anything, it would help people in these professions feel more comfortable.

- Those aren't holes in my socks, those are vents. You should make vents in your socks, otherwise your feet will stink.

- Most people rarely wash their jackets, shoes and hats. The very things which they wear the most are the things they wash the least.

- Why do women get so caught up in their outfits? Honestly, most men don't care about clothing. We prefer women with no clothing.

- What are the rules for washing jeans? I believe jeans can be worn up to five days because washing them too often causes significant fading.

Of course the rules drastically change if you wear jeans in a public place, like the subway or airplane. In those cases jeans must be incinerated after a single use.

- Ever notice how women feel more powerful when they walk loudly on hardwood floors with high heels or boots?

- For some reason most people are willing to listen to the ideas of someone wearing a suit.

- If I iron my jeans does that make me a lesser man?

- Vests and shorts are brilliant because the length of your arms and legs does not matter. With shirts and pants there are too many dimensions. If I ever launch a clothing company, I will make only vests and shorts.

- Why do I debate which shirt to wear? It's like I'm complicating my life. Why not just buy ten copies of the best shirt and wear it every single day? I feel like the only reason I wear different colored shirts and pants is to signal to other people that I wash my clothes.

- Ever hear of *ugly sweaters*? Can you imagine being in charge of designing the ugliest sweaters? That's like telling someone to do their job as poorly as possible. Imagine the job interview; "Can you please explain to us how you are the least qualified person for this position?"

- Why don't adults wear shoes with lights? It seems practical.

- I hate when I get a wet spot on the front of my pants from washing dishes. I get so defensive. I have to tell everyone, "I was washing dishes."

- Ever buy a shirt with tags in like eight different languages? I think to myself, "These people in the sweatshops are smarter than me; I can barely speak *one* language."

- Why are clothing tags usually on the back of garments? It's impossible to read the labels without spinning my head 180 degrees. For shirts, the tag should be upside down and on the front. Then I could lift up the shirt and read the tag.

- I once bought a shirt which had a little scissor icon showing how to cut the label off. If I'm supposed to cut the label off, then why did they sew it on?

- Why do women buy expensive purses? I just assume they're counterfeit.

- I hate that when I buy new clothes I need to wash them before wearing them. It makes buying new clothes anticlimactic.

- People are so conscious of the brands on their jackets; it's like it helps them identify their clique. Do you belong to the Patagonia clique, Mountain Hardware clique or North Face clique?

- The invention of the shoe was as significant to neanderthals as the car was to the modern age. It revolutionized transportation completely. Without footwear, walking on sharp rocks or snow was painful. It also caused restaurants to boom, as neanderthals could comply with the sign *No shoes, No shirt, No service.*

- Why do people get excited about dressing up? It's like they're putting on a Halloween costume.

- When you wear something and you ask someone how it looks, do they ever say that it looks terrible? Of course not. If you want an honest opinion, seek the advice of a five-year-old. They're blunt.

- Why do we have entire closets full of clothing? Why not just have two pairs of pants and two shirts? I have shirts I have not worn for over a year. Why do I keep them?

- Has someone ever complimented you by saying you look professional? Isn't it unprofessional to comment on a person's looks in the workplace? Unless your job is to model, what you wear is technically irrelevant.

- Why can't lawyers wear gym shorts and go barefoot to court? Aren't the scales of justice blind? If anything I want my attorney wearing athletic gear. I want to know he or she has the stamina to win a long case.

- People spend way too much time thinking about what to wear. Just wear black. Wearing black is considered fashionable and requires zero effort.

- Why do meteorologists announce the weather forecast in numeric terms? I just want to know what to wear. Rather than saying that it's going to be forty degrees today, they should just say, "Wear a heavy sweater, hat and pants."

- What's wrong with wearing a jacket indoors? Who cares if it's called a jackct or a sweater? Why can't I just be comfortable?

- Why do motorcyclists wear leather jackets? Are they unaware that water shrinks leather and that it can rain outside?

- Why do they call it a *sports coat*? You can't play sports in it.

- If my banker is wearing a very expensive suit, does that mean I'm getting screwed on banking fees? I would much rather have my banker wear tattered clothes.

- The *power tie* is a euphemism for an obnoxious bib.

Coffee

- Ice cream trucks are common, so why don't we have coffee trucks too? Though I suppose not many people would like to hear loud music on their street at five o'clock in the morning.

- I'm not a fan of pretentious coffee shops that charge eight dollars for fancy coffees with names that are twenty words long.

- I think people go to coffee houses just to people-watch. It's where you make fun of people from a distance. Criticizing strangers is the fastest way to build your self esteem.

- I've always wanted to be a hero and stop a robbery in process. In my mind, the ideal scenario is one where I toss my hot coffee on the robber and save the day.

Coffee vs Tea

- When I drink tea, I think about the American colonists dumping tea in Boston harbor to resist the British; it seems stuffy. When I drink coffee, I think of wild Colombian drug lords, which is exciting.

- If you want to make a billion dollars, invent coffee that doesn't stain teeth.

- Ever meet people who rave about using coffee grinds for gardening? It's as if they buy the coffee not to drink it, but rather to dump it out.

- I sometimes wonder about coffee bean fraud. How am I to know if these beans really came from Ethiopia or the mountains of Jamaica? Who's to say they didn't come from Florida?

- Why is there *tea time*, but there's no *coffee time*?

- Why do coffee tables exist? It seems like an excessively large piece of furniture to hold a cup. There should be a coffee column or mini coffee tower to hold the drink. And why is there a teaspoon but no coffee spoon?

- When I go to the gas station, I know the octane of my gasoline. Shouldn't coffee and tea have a similar caffeine rating?

College & Education

- Why do people buy college shirts for their babies? Who do they think they're fooling? The kid can barely walk and they expect me to believe it has a degree? I doubt the kid can spell his or her name.

- If colleges are preparing students for the *real world*, then why do they grade papers? I've never had a paper graded at work. In the real world, the closest thing to grades is a paycheck. If colleges really want to prepare students for the real world, then they should pay students a generous amount each time they write a great paper.

- If colleges advocate that students volunteer to help their communities, then why do professors charge for teaching?

- The biggest difference between life before college and after college is the use of drink coasters.

- Why do the smartest kids get all the scholarships? It's the least intelligent kids who need the most help.

- Grade schools excel at encouraging reckless lifestyles. That's why school buses have no seatbelts.

- If your kid gets a detention at school, isn't that a good thing? Doesn't it mean more hours of free education?

Construction

- *Men Working* construction signs: are they meant to remind the workers of what they're supposed to be doing? Or is that to remind me of what work looks like?

- I love the identity of being a tough man and doing home construction. But when I actually start doing work, I realize it's very tiring and it takes four times longer than I could ever imagine.

Cooking

- Why do people need so many kitchen knives? Who cuts with more than one knife at a time?

- I love it when I'm cooking and someone says, "Don't overcook it." As if I *intended* to overcook anything? Great advice. Thanks.

- If you cook dinner and ask someone if they like it, they will feel compelled to lie and give a false compliment. You can only trust unsolicited compliments.

- Who are the fools that invented the dry measuring cup and the liquid measuring cup? Why do we have the same names for different measurements?

- I hate reading cooking recipes. I feel like I'm taking orders from a stranger.

Coronavirus

- The nice thing about Coronavirus is that women don't expect to go to restaurants. Going to the park or beach is sufficient. Guys around the world are thrilled they don't have to spend money on fancy dinners or drinks.

- I used to get a rush from watching action movies. But now with Coronavirus being so dangerous, most action movies seem lame. Real life is far more interesting than the movies.

- One of the greatest joys of Coronavirus is that it gives us the isolation necessary to try new haircuts. Mohawks, dyed hair, shaved heads, spikes. Whatever your fantasy, use the quarantine as the time to test it out. Grow a beard in the shape of tusks, nobody cares!

- Life under Coronavirus is like an alternate reality. This world is so bizarre now that if extraterrestrial aliens landed here, I wouldn't be shocked.

- In the past dating was pretty simple: I might want to review someone's credit and check references with their past three exes. But now it seems reasonable to ask for Coronavirus test results before dating. Meh.

- True story: I was dating this woman and I gave her some N-95 masks. She thought it was romantic.

- Dating a person while keeping six feet of social distance is like trying to build a fire with blocks of ice.

Credit

- Why do all these credit card companies offer points? Points, points, points, points. All I hear about are these points. You would think they were running a video game.

- I love how when I spend my money, I'm "earning" cash back on my credit card. What a euphemism.

Dating

- I've met a number of women who were nervous about the first date. I suppose dating safety is a fair concern in this day and age. I often tell these women that they're welcome to bring a gun on the date. I assume that would make them feel safer, but my good intentions are often misunderstood.

- Why is it that people rarely use calendars to keep track of date nights? For work I always schedule upcoming meetings. But I feel like for dates, most ladies need a confirmation text twenty-four hours in advance. I usually text, "Will you be attending your 6:00PM date tomorrow? Text Y for Yes or N to unsubscribe."

- Text messaging makes life so concise; we forget the formalities and skip right to the chase. Instead of asking a woman how she's doing, I can just text, "WUMM?" ("Will you marry me?")

- Boring dates feel like an interview. Most ladies ask the same questions: "Where did you go to school? How many siblings do you have? Where do your parents live?" But who really cares? If a woman has no siblings or one hundred siblings, does it matter? I find the best dates are the ones where I learn the least information about her and we crack jokes the whole time.

- The best thing about dating is that when I go to a restaurant the host no longer announces, "Table for a party of *just* one?"

- I wish I could write reviews of the women I've dated. It would be great if they could do the same for me. Feedback is how we improve in life. Rather than breaking up with someone and not leaving a reason, I would write, "She borrowed my favorite sweatshirt and returned it unwashed."

- It amazes me how people are hesitant to spend ten dollars per month to subscribe to an online dating site. Isn't finding the love of your life worth more than ten dollars?

- True story: I once met a girl on Tinder who was a real estate agent. I asked if she wanted to go out. She asked if I would buy a house.

- Asking a woman to split the check on a date is fun. I never know what to expect.

- When people talk about restaurants for a date, they'll say, "That place looks good." But in reality the architecture of the building and the taste of the food have nothing in common.

- With online dating sites, I've got some rules: I don't date women who have pictures of themselves skydiving, riding motorcycles or riding horses. They're outside my risk tolerance.

- Online dating demonstrates the height of civilization. In a nanosecond I swipe right or left on a picture, choosing the woman with whom I want to spend my entire life. If I can choose my life partner in a nanosecond, then how can any other major life decision take more than a nanosecond?

- The most confusing online dating profile picture is the group shot with friends. What if I'm not attracted to the woman on the dating app, but I'm attracted to her friends? Is it okay for me to ask for her friend's number?

- I feel shallow choosing women on dating apps based mostly on looks. Would it be less shallow of me to ask for credit reports, bank statements, pay stubs, a college transcript and personal essay?

- They should make a dating application for gold diggers. Rather than making women guess how much money a man has, why not just show their bank account in real time? Filter guys by net worth? What's wrong with being honest?

- I'm not good at dating long-term planners. How can I plan a date three days in advance when I'm not sure what I'm wearing tomorrow?

- The name of the woman I date is important. I refuse to date any woman with the same name as my close relatives. I also refuse to date women who have porn star names, like Candi or Destinee.

- The reason online dating is so appealing is because people look younger, have better names and are more interesting. It's expected that you lie about your age and that your photos are a couple years old. If you don't, then you're putting yourself at a huge disadvantage. Online dating is about projecting your best fake self.

- When you give away your heart, it means you've fallen in love with someone right? So it's good to be heartless, right?

- You'll know you've been online-dating too long when you walk by people and you start swiping right or left.

- Most men struggle with their body image for online dating. We assume we're perfect 10's and try to chase women out of our league. It's a delicate topic that most men never discuss.

- True story: The most interesting online dating picture I've ever seen was of a woman pulling a tractor trailer truck with a rope. I swiped left.

- True story: I once dated a woman and she was venting to me about her terrible day at work. She told me, "I'm so mad, I'm going to mail them an envelope full of glitter."

- In online dating profiles people clearly pose for the pictures. Men know how to make their biceps look larger by pressing them against their chest. Women know that a picture from an elevated angle with puckered lips makes them look thinner. Despite knowing these tricks, most people both use them and simultaneously still fall for them.

- I'm worried about dating during a cyber attack. So as a contingency, I'm launching a new line of t-shirts that say "Swipe." Then as I walk in public, if I woman swipes right, I'll know she's interested.

- What's the rule on escaping a terrible date? How many minutes must I stay?

- When on a date, why do women ask about my occupation? I'm trying to date them romantically.

I'm not trying to network professionally.

- Why do people talk about their exes on dates? It's like when you're driving down the highway at eighty miles per hour and someone asks, "Have you had any good car accidents lately?"

- These are my basic rules to dating. I'm pretty certain these are obvious and universal:

    - Thou shall not reschedule the first date. If a woman tries to reschedule, it means I'm not her priority or she's a disaster.

    - Thou shall not date women who own chihuahuas. What grown man wants to be a servant to a tiny dog?

    - Thou shall not date women with the same name as a recent ex-girlfriend.

    - Thou shall only date women with positive Uber and AirBNB ratings.

    - Thou shall only date polite women. If a woman does not say, "Thank you" to the waiter when a meal or drink is served, then she is rude. There will be no second date.

o Thou shall not date women who talk excessively about their exes. If a woman talks about her ex for more than fourteen seconds during the first date, then there will be no second date.

o Thou shall not date women who order the most expensive item on the menu. If she orders the most expensive item, then there will be no second date.

o Thou shall not date women who send a drink back to the bar (on the first date) because it isn't mixed right. High maintenance women are never worth the hassle.

o Thou shall not date women who conveniently excuse themselves to the restroom when the bill is placed on the table.

Drinking

- As a tough man I keep my finger nails cut short. But this makes it impossible to open a can of beer by myself. There's nothing more emasculating as a man than asking a woman with long nails to open my drink.

- Why do people always curl their pinky finger while drinking?

- If the bartender refuses to charge drinks to your library card, then you shouldn't be driving.

- Drinking isn't bad for my memory. It helps me forget bad memories and make room for new ones.

- How can people claim that poor decisions are only made while drinking? After all, the decision to drink starts with a sober mind.

- It's true drinking destroys the liver, but it also creates healthcare jobs. So if someone asks you to stop drinking, just think about how many doctors and nurses will be out of work.

- Why do drunk drivers get free food and free housing in jail? Doesn't that just help them save money for beer?

- If alcohol is an "adult beverage" then why does it make adults act childish?

- Alcohol is used to disinfect cuts and sterilize medical instruments. So how can it be unhealthy to consume it?

- I've designed an excellent home-based test to determine if I've had too much to drink. It's called the *Hot French Fry Test*. I drop a French fry in the hot oven. If I can remove it without getting burned, then I might be safe to drive. But if I get burned while trying to remove it, then I've had too much to drink.

- I think police should set a new style of trap to catch drunk drivers. A simple sign stating *Free beer at the police station* with an arrow should work.

- Cars should have a Captcha test to make certain drivers are not drunk.

Dogs

- I feel like dogs have more rights than humans. A dog can take a leak anywhere it wants.

- Have you ever seen a dog vacuum a house? Of course not. They never have to clean. It's a good life.

- True story: I once saw a lady walk into Home Depot while carrying her tiny dog. It didn't seem right. Tiny dogs don't belong in tough stores.

- Dogs don't shower daily. That's gross.

- A couple times I've had dogs aggressively bark at me while showing their teeth. Then the dog owner said, "It's okay, this dog is friendly." I think some dog owners are delusional.

- If a guy sees a woman walking a puppy and strikes up a conversation, trust me, the guy has zero interest in the puppy. He's just trying to hit on the woman.

- Lots of people want dogs, but they don't have time to care for them. Pets should be rentable by the hour.

- I don't understand how dog "lovers" can wrap leashes around dogs' necks.

Dogs Are Better Than Cats

- Cougars are women who prey on innocent young men. Therefore, cats are evil.

- Cat burglars are criminals. Therefore, cats are evil.

- I always hear about the crazy cat lady, but I never hear about the crazy dog lady? Why is that?

- Nothing kills the romantic mood more than a cat digging in its litter box. If you want to stay single, get a cat.

Email

- Aren't you sick of those emails stating, "Congratulations, you've just won 5 million dollars"? I win so often, I don't even reply.

- I miss those chain email threats about the government charging taxes on email. I haven't seen them in like ten years.

Environment

- I'm not too lazy to mow the lawn. I'm an active environmentalist supporting nature.

- How can paper bags be better for the environment than plastic bags? Trees are killed to produce paper bags, while plastic bags are made from inanimate oil. Is it better to kill living trees or to remove chemicals from the ground?

- I care about the environment and I don't like oil polluting the ground. So to help remove oil from the earth I drive a gas-guzzling SUV.

- How can coastal land erosion be bad? It's natural.

- Why does it bother environmentalists when the drinking water is polluted? Doesn't that mean that fewer people will have water to drink and ultimately there will be fewer people to pollute the world?

- How dare environmentalists say that the fishermen are killing off the fish? If the world's fish population decreases then fishermen will be out of work, right? If anything, fishermen care more about the world's fish population than anyone else. No one has a greater financial interest in the success of the fish population than fishermen.

- How can environmentalists claim dams are bad for the environment? Dams save water.

- It's not a swamp; it's a wildlife marsh. It's not a dump; it's a recycling center.

- I wouldn't say we're killing the trees. I prefer to say we're removing the old ones to make room for the young ones.

- Why aren't you happy that Antarctica is melting? Once it's fully melted we'll be able to ship goods by boat from Asia to North America via the North Pole. This shipping route will be shorter and therefore save valuable oil. If you want to help conserve oil, you should celebrate the end of Antarctica.

- The flaw to most environmental studies is that they focus all their research on proving the existence of pollution. Yet they fail to allocate an equal amount of time *disproving* the existence of pollution.. So their research is inherently biased. I demand that the researchers allocate equal funding and time to the opposite side of the issue.

- Pollution is good for real estate values. The more we pollute, the more rare and valuable clean land becomes.

- How can important natural resources be depleted? It's not as if these resources are physically leaving Earth's atmosphere. The resources are just temporarily displaced.

- How can scientists claim they are trying to save the environment? If scientists didn't cure so many diseases, mankind would not overpopulate Earth. If scientists didn't discover nuclear power, we wouldn't pollute the oceans with radioactive waste. Science is quite obviously the leading cause of environmental devastation. The best way to save the Earth is by ending science.

- Do you really think wildlife organizations want to protect endangered species? If their employees succeed, then the species will no longer be endangered. If the species is no longer endangered then what will these people do for work? They'll be fired. Doesn't it sound bad if the goal of an organization is to fire all their employees?

- When people recycle cans and bottles they assume there is no waste created, so they use even more cans and bottles. But in reality this is increasing the consumption of resources.

Therefore, recycling is bad.

- How dare environmentalists criticize me for drinking bottled water because the plastic bottle pollutes? It's no different than drinking a soda or sports drink. In fact, drinking bottled water is much healthier than drinking soda or a sports drink. I will not apologize for living a healthy lifestyle. If environmentalists want to criticize me for drinking bottled water then they should be consistent: They should criticize everyone who uses any kind of plastic container.

- I invented a new eco-friendly vehicle which is powered by water and sugar. It's called a bicycle.

Fish

- Why do fishing hobbyists use fish finders? If you want to take a high tech approach to finding a fish, just buy a fish online or drive to a fish market.

- What in the world are salmon thinking when they swim up shallow creeks to spawn? It's like 300,000 fish agree to beat up their bodies and jump straight into the mouths of grizzly bears. This irrational behavior seems to disprove the theory of evolution.

Food

- How can bacon possibly be bad for me? Wild pigs can run thirty miles per hour and they're made of bacon.

- I think some of the smartest people on Earth work in the fast food industry flipping burgers. These people are selling junk food for high prices. I can't even sell healthy food at a low price.

- True story: I bought some lemon juice in a bottle and the label read, "Made from real lemons." I should hope so!

- Where did this avocado craze come from? It seems like for the past ten years, everyone has been obsessed with avocados. They've been around for thousands of years. Why are millennials so obscsscd?

- True story: I was watching a television show about the dangers of junk food and fast food. The show was then interrupted by commercials for M&Ms and McDonald's.

- If you're at a friend's house and you're offered pizza, is it okay to turn it down and help yourself to anything in the kitchen?

- Why is it that so many of the things we enjoy are unhealthy?   Alcohol destroys the liver, coffee gives us high blood pressure and chocolate causes cavities. Such a cruel world.

- Why do people always serve cheeseburgers with the cheese on top of the burger? To truly enjoy the cheese the burger must be eaten upside down. Cheeseburgers should always be served with the cheese beneath the meat. Case closed.

- Energy bars are just candy bars with better marketing.

- Eating at restaurants is so lame. We ask for our food, sit in our chairs and then it's brought to us. Whatever happened to the days of the hunters and gathers? Whatever happened to the times when we had to run and chase down our food?

- Why do farm animals get to take steroids but humans can't? It just doesn't seem fair.

- Ever try to please an entire group of people when ordering takeout? It's impossible. You get vegans, celiacs, carnivores, paleo people - so many different groups. Asking a group of people what they want for dinner just leads to forced compromise. My new philosophy is that if you don't like what I make, then you're free to use my phone and order yourself some takeout.

- What's wrong with eating food that fell on the floor? Vegetables are grown on the ground, outside and in manure.

- Hamburgers and steak are the same thing so why isn't the cost identical? If anything, hamburgers should be more expensive because it requires machinery to grind the meat up.

- Pizza restaurants are so mainstream. I feel like there's no emotional connection when I order my food. I think there should be pizza dealerships where you enter, sit down for a drink and speak to a pizza consultant about your unique pizza needs. The pizza consultant would then ask about your party's size, the occasion, beverage preferences, venue, group dietary restrictions, music and dress code. Based on this info a pizza could then be paired properly.

- How can someone say they're eating *all-natural* pasta? Does spaghetti grow naturally in the wild?

- Microwaved pizza always gets soggy and gross. It should be forbidden by governmental decree.

- There are rules to food. One of those is that oranges cannot be eaten straight from the refrigerator..

- How can you honestly say that vegetables are good for me? You know pigs get fat from eating vegetables. Vegetables are the primary ingredient used to make bacon. Vegetables are obviously unhealthy.

- Serving food is all about euphemisms. Old apple juice is fresh hard cider. Strips of unhealthy fat are savory bacon. Uncooked steak is steak tartare. Raw fish is sushi. Spoiled milk is aged cheese.

- If you serve a kid pizza, then why not give him or her a beer? They're both made of water, sugar, wheat and yeast. It's pretty much the same thing.

- When I eat brie cheese, am I supposed to peel off that outer casing or eat it? I wish they included an instruction manual.

- How dare people insult me for putting too much salt in their food. Salt was a form of currency during the Roman Empire. In fact the word *salary* is derived from the Latin word *salārium* which means *salt money*.

- Why do vegetarians constantly preach to me that I shouldn't eat meat? I eat a lot less meat than most lions. Vegetarians should focus their efforts on lions.

- If most people in the world can eat for less than a dollar per day, does that mean I'm getting ripped off?

- I love Thanksgiving. It gives me a chance to utilize all my belt notches.

Friends

- Why is it that when I attend a party, strangers always ask how I know our mutual friend. It's as if there's this social media blockchain. If I met someone on the bus in grade school or randomly at a business conference, what difference does it make?

- When a friend is late by ten minutes, should I make him or her wait ten minutes before speaking?

Furniture

- Why are there massive tags on furniture? Do I really need to know the material is recycled and it's illegal in California to remove the tag? Don't lawmakers have more important things to do?

- Why do people bother with coasters? What's the point of having a table if you can't leave things on it?

- Why do people use decorative pillows on their beds? Who are they fooling? Nobody really needs eight pillows on their bed. It's as if they think their bed is being featured in a home decor catalog.

- Why don't people wash their couch cushions? Seems pretty gross that they get sat on all year, yet never cleaned.

- Why do people use down pillows? Sleeping on the feathers of dead birds seems unsanitary. It's further compounded by the fact that the down pillows are virtually impossible to wash.

- Why is it such a big deal to buy a used mattress? Most people think it's gross, yet they stay in hotel beds which are used by thousands of people.

- Why do people bother buying formal furniture? It seems like the fanciest furniture is that which gets used the least.

- Book shelves, tables, desks, beds, chairs and trunks can all be built from milk crates. I only advocate milk crate furniture.

- Who reads the labels on furniture? Do they really expect me to hold my couch in the air so I can read the label underneath?
Grocery Stores

- Grocery stores have a terrible name. The word *gross* is repulsive. Someone should get on this and rename them.

- What's up with those obnoxious *Member Discount* cards at grocery stores? If you don't use them the price is like fifty percent higher than advertised. I refuse to keep them. I prefer to ask the clerk to provide me with a new card which I then immediately throw away.

- Why do people love free samples at the grocery store? The sample could be worth five cents and taste terrible yet people wait in line for fifteen minutes.

Greetings

- I find it invasive when a stranger asks me how I'm doing. I don't even know his or her name, and yet he or she has the audacity to ask for my most personal feelings?

- Greetings are lies. At the supermarket:

> Cashier: "How are you?"

> Me: "I'm doing well. How are you?"

> Cashier: "I'm doing well, too. Thanks for asking."

Why do we bother with this ritual? The person in line right before me just asked the same questions. I already heard the answers and the answers aren't even honest. The cashier likely hates his or her job, and would much rather be at home. Likewise, I hate shopping and handing over my money.

God

- God seems like an ambitious fellow. Creating the Earth seems like a lot of work. If I were God I would just spend all day playing with lightning bolts, tornadoes and tsunamis.

- How long did God plan to build the Earth? Where did he or she get the idea? I'm really curious about the project management map and planning.

Government

- Why are state capitol buildings so nice? They're often made of gold and marble. The last thing I want to do is walk into the state capitol and be reminded of how my tax dollars are being wasted on such lavish buildings.

- I'm impressed that the founders of America wrote the *Declaration of Independence*. They had really nice handwriting.

- It's not called "Begging for money," it's called "Applying for a grant."

- I'm not saying that the President intentionally uses a weather machine to cause hurricanes. I'm just saying it's awfully suspicious he's always on the scene right after they happen.

- I love how the government refers to *Tax* as *Revenue* rather than *Extortion fees*.

- I'm not saying the government is run by the mob, but rather that the mob is run like the government. They both maintain monopolies, charge people for protection and kill the opposition.

- I'm glad the city hasn't paved the potholes on my street. It prevents people from driving on my street and keeps it quieter. An ineffective government is best.

- It's okay to lie when you're being "politically correct."

- Guns are far less dangerous than candy bars. Only 114,000 Americans are shot each year, while over 300,000 Americans die from obesity. If you want to save lives, you should confiscate the candy bars and give people guns.

- I think there is a misconception that people in the government are stupid and bad with money. In actuality they're getting paid to do nothing. That's genius and financially savvy.

- If we want to keep religion and government separate, should we stop placing our faith in the government?

Guns

- Why do people have glass gun display cabinets? It's like dangling a block of cash from a string to tease a robber. It just attracts attention.

- When doing demolition work on the house, I prefer my twelve gauge shotgun over a sledge hammer.

- It's amazing that any kid in America can buy explosive gasoline without any permits, yet guns require background checks.

Gyms

- The only reason men do yoga is to be surrounded by beautiful women. Let's be honest, men don't care about their own flexibility.

- When I say someone is "as strong as an ant," that's a compliment because ants can carry fifty times their body weight.

- Who invents the crazy machines at the gym? I mean these things have ropes, pulleys, weights and bands coming from all directions. It seems like the machines have come from some medieval torture catalog.

- Am I supposed to use the chemical spray at the gym *before* I exercise or *after* I exercise? Let's be honest, most people don't clean things *after* use, so why should I feel guilty about spraying the equipment *before* use?

- I have no patience for people who stand around the gym occupying the equipment but not actually using it.. These are the people who bring their duffle bag onto the gym floor and have a giant protein shake in their hands. They're so dramatic. Why can't they just use their machine and move on?

- If he's so tough then why does he even need to use weights? Weights are used by weak people who want to become stronger.

- Ever see those people in the gym who are desperate for attention? You know, the guy or gal who throws dumbbells down. As if using gravity and making a ton of noise is a workout?

- I was thinking about working out my toes muscles. I think that's an overlooked muscle group.

- Of course I could lift with my legs and not with my back, but then when will my back muscles have a chance to work out?

Haircuts & Hair

- Unless I'm using a mirror I never see my hair. So why should I care what my hair looks like? I should not be responsible for choosing my own haircut.

- Whenever I get a bad haircut I assume everyone will notice, but in reality nobody cares.

- I feel like the man-bun is cultural appropriation from sumo wrestlers. It seems disrespectful to wear it if a person isn't a sumo wrestler.

Health

- It seems like everyone has a sickness now. If you're sad then you have depression. If you're bored then you've got attention deficit disorder. And if you're happy, then you're delusional.

- Have you ever been sick and someone said you should "drink lots of fluids." Fluids? Am I a car going in for an oil change?

- Ever meet someone who is smug about their diet and claims to not eat processed food? Then you ask about their diet and they openly admit to using a blender to process it.

- How can it be unhealthy for people to be fat? Blue whales are covered in a one-foot-thicker layer of fat. They migrate 16,000 miles per year. It sounds like they're in great shape.

- Some people complain that if you take vitamins they dissolve. Isn't that the point? Don't you want to dissolve the nutrients into your bloodstream?

- How can a doctor understand my health better than me? The doctor will only see me for a few minutes, but I've known myself for decades.

- He's not a drug dealer. He's an unlicensed pharmacist.

- How can a vegetarian diet possibly be healthy? Elephants are vegetarians yet they weigh thousands of pounds and are slow. Cheetahs are carnivores yet they're lean and super fast. Do you want to be fat like an elephant or lean like a cheetah?

- It's great that 1/3 of Americans are obese. It means they're not starving. We should be so lucky. Now the question is, how do we feed the other 2/3 of Americans?

- The problem with humanity is we don't have enough natural predators to chase us and keep us in shape. To improve public health we should re-release tyrannosauruses into the streets.

- I'm not saying hospitals kill people, I just think it's awfully suspicious how many people die when they go to hospitals. If you want to live a long life, avoid the hospital.

- The only war I support is the war on plaque and cavities.

- I tell kids that adults never eat candy bars for dinner. But what I don't tell them is that adults secretly eat candy bars for breakfast, lunch and their midafternoon snack.

85

Holidays

- Who has the authority to create new holidays? How do I become a member of this secret group?

- Halloween is a time to reveal our suppressed alter egos. It's also the one day of the year where using black lights is acceptable for adults.

Homes

- I don't understand how people can complain that their homes are too small? When I look up at their ceilings I just see unused space.

- Have you ever had your fire alarm beep at 2:00 AM to indicate a low battery? The timing makes the alert completely ineffective; at 2:00 AM, I'm so tired, I don't care if the house burns down.

- Who invented the sliding door? They always break.

- When people buy houses, they are always excited about getting the best view possible. Yet they rarely go to their attic, which always has the best view.

Honesty

- Have Americans become too sensitive? Is it better to be honest and offend someone, or to lie and be agreeable? That's why I respect little kids. They're brutally honest. If they don't like food, it gets thrown against the wall.

- Sometimes it's best not to speak the truth. If you think your friend has a really hot spouse, it's best to keep this opinion to yourself.

Hotels

- Hotels often have windows that don't open. I guess they're afraid someone might want fresh air.

- Staying in a hotel makes me feel like an important business person. If you want to feel important you should stay in a hotel.

- When I stay in hotels I get really excited about the free continental breakfast and coffee; I really want to get my money's worth with that coffee. I'll drink the coffee even if it's terrible so I have the satisfaction of having gotten a good deal on the hotel.

- I always want to get the full value at a hotel; I check in early and leave as late as possible.

- You never know what's happened to the hotel furniture. It's best not to think about it.

- Ever stay in a hotel room where there is a door that connects adjacent rooms? Those doors freak me out. I always worry about my neighbor unlocking it in the middle of the night.

- The continental breakfast always sounds so wonderful, but in truth it is usually mediocre.

- I like to tip the cleaning crew at the hotel, but I never carry cash. What am I supposed to do? Find an ATM and return to the hotel? Seems like a lot of work.

- If I leave a tip for the hotel cleaning staff, is the person who cleaned the room going to actually receive it? Or does it just go to the person who happened to open the door first after I leave?

- What should you do with the hotel towels? Is it okay to leave them on the floor? What is proper used-towel protocol?

- Does the hotel cleaning crew prefer no tip and a clean room? Or a big tip and a messy room?

Household

- Lawns are for people who want to over complicate their lives. That's why people plant grass which they mow for years. If they valued their time, they would just plant moss.

- It seems like the only time I see people outside is when they're maintaining their yard. When was the last time you saw a homeowner playing in his or her yard?

- Why is it that home improvement projects take forever? I had to assemble a bunk bed, which sounds like a two minute project. But in actuality it took two trips to the hardware store and two hours. When working on a home improvement project, you should always assume it's going to take sixty times longer than expected.

- Am I the only person who is territorial about their laundry scent? If someone does my laundry using a different detergent, I can't wear it. I feel like I'm wearing someone else's clothes.

Human Body

- Why do we compliment people with statements like, "You're tall" or "You have nice hair"? As if the person had any control over his or her genetics? No work was done to gain these traits.

- Toes are ugly. Why do we have them? I wish I had flippers or wheels instead. At least those would be more practical.

- Why do humans only have one heart? It seems like this is a design flaw resulting in a potential single point of failure. We have two lungs, eyes, ears, arms and feet, yet just one heart?

Hunting

- Once hunting season is over, poaching season starts. I like poaching season because it lasts longer, has no rules and no limit.

- Hunters often wear fluorescent orange camouflage assuming that deer can't see it. Who figured this out? How many deer were in the focus group?

> Marketing strategist to deer: "We're making this new bright orange hunting jacket. Can you see it?"
>
> Deer, convincingly: "Oh no, I can't see him. That large hunter with the 30-06 rifle looks like a tree with branches. I definitely can't see him from twenty-five miles away. He blends right in."

- True story: I was at Cabela's in Maine and I overheard this couple buying a gun. The woman said she'd sell a couple of her hand bags so they could buy the gun on layaway.

Investing

- Why would I ever hire a financial planner? Aren't the best ones retired?

- When I choose a financial planner, is okay to ask his or her net worth?

- When I make a mistake on my computer, I can usually press, "Ctrl+Z" or "Command+Z" to undo it. Why doesn't my stock brokerage account have the same "Edit/Undo" feature?

- Most companies advertise sales weeks in advance. I wish the stock exchanges would advertise sales on stock *before* the prices crash.

- Investment commercials make it seem so exciting to sock away money during your youth in exchange for material assets in your senior years.

- Investing in the stock market sounds like a video game where the score is kept in points and not dollars. "The market is up fifty points today…"

Jewelry

- True story: I once bought a gold bracelet. I asked the jeweler how he knew it was 10K. He told me it was 10K because 10K was written on the bracelet. I then wrote *10K* on a piece of paper and explained that writing *10K* on paper does not make it gold.

- I was wearing a gold bracelet and a woman told me it was terrible for the environment. I told her that I agreed and that's why I was wearing it. I wanted to generate awareness for the environmental devastation caused by gold mining.

- I don't understand the purpose of owning jewelry. If you wear it in public you can get robbed. If you wear it at home, you're less likely to be robbed, but nobody will see it. So why even bother owning it?

Kids

- Every new parent should enroll in a hostage negotiation class before having kids.

- Kids can be cute, especially when they're not mine.

- Most kids haven't fallen for the expensive organic food trend. They're frugal and prefer deep fried chicken nuggets over grass fed filet mignon.

- Kids make it easy for parents to find them. Just follow the trail of broken crayons, food scraps and toys.

- If you want your kids to eat vegetables, just change the name of things. Refer to thinly sliced carrots as "orange cookies."

- You've got to admire the imagination of kids. It's similar to drunk people. Something as simple as a couch can become an airplane.

- Who are these crazy engineers that design playgrounds? A swing set is basically a catapult. And yet, we build these things on school grounds and encourage kids to use them?

- I sometimes wonder what Gandhi did on the playground in second grade.

Law

- If you're mad that lobbyists are corrupting our laws, then hire a lobbyist to ban lobbying.

- How come the American Bar Association doesn't allow indicted criminals to become lawyers? Don't convicted felons have the most real world experience?

- Why does the law require that people wear seatbelts? If a person wants to go flying through the windshield, can't we just respect that personal choice?

- *Rock, Paper, Scissors* is a great way for kids to solve problems. I wonder if *paper* is symbolic for laws beating brute force?

- Aren't laws supposed to be constant? If the laws can be changed, then what's the point in having them?

- I would assume that after one year, all the laws of the entire world could be written. Yet somehow, after two hundred years lawmakers keep making new ones.

- It's good that laws can't be understood by the layman. Otherwise they could be followed and attorneys would be out of work.

Libraries

- I think most librarians are illiterate. That's why they stack the books on shelves horizontally so the titles on the spines can't be read. In English we read right to left, not top to bottom. If librarians were literate they would stack books in vertical piles.

- I suppose it's good that homeless people hangout in libraries. Hopefully they're sharpening their minds, or reminding students why it's important to study.

Mail

- Receiving mail is an unnecessary daily chore. If a piece of information can take a couple of days to get to me, why not let it sit for a year? I wish the post office offered *Last Class* stamps, where the letter would take two hundred years to arrive.

- My friends are shocked when I mail them stuff. They're amazed that I know how to mail packages. Mailing stuff is a dying art.

- True story: My neighbor's mother died and I accidentally sent a condolence card using a *Celebrate!* stamp.

- Since junk mail ends up in the trash, why does the post office bother delivering it? They should just collect the stamp revenue and incinerate the mail.

- I heard the post office will stop delivering mail on Saturday. Is that a bad thing? Doesn't it just delay my bills? Why not just stop delivering all together?

- Why do people pay for post office boxes? Doesn't it cost the United States Post Office more money to deliver to each house than to drop off mail inside their own building?

102

Millennials

- You might be a millennial if you do paddle-board yoga.

- You might be a millennial if you have $250,000 in college loans.

- You might be a millennial if you eat avocado toast.

Money

- I didn't lose my wallet. I just hid it in a location so safe even I don't know where it is.

- Why is it that non-profit churches, universities and museums have the best architecture and most expensive buildings? Is the high cost of these buildings the very reason why these groups show no profit?

- What's the difference between an unemployed person and retired person? Word choice.

- I don't own old useless junk. I own antiques.

- True story: I once went to a store which had the sign, "No credit, bad credit, no problem! We accept cash."

- I'm not saying that all criminals are bankers. But both criminals and bankers both possess money that doesn't belong to them. It seems suspicious.

- The house isn't derelict; it's a historic landmark with character.

- In the winter, opening your windows to let the heat out isn't wasting money. It's creating jobs for the oil industry. Jobs are good. You should open your windows all winter long.

- That house isn't tiny. By Manhattan standards, it's a mansion.

- Why would you ever want to amass a fortune and lots of assets? You can't take it with you to the grave and the government is going to tax it. If anything, you should amass as much debt as possible.

- My investments aren't losing money; I'm just investing long term - like two or three thousand years.

- I didn't forget to pay the electric bill. I just prefer the smell and flicker of candles.

- I'm not paying 20% interest on my credit cards because I have bad credit. I'm paying 20% because I'm tipping for excellent customer service.

- I didn't lose money in the stock market; I donated to strangers.

Movies

- Who in their right mind buys a gallon of popcorn at the movie theater? And why must such massive snacks be consumed while watching movies? It's not like running a marathon; It takes zero energy to watch a movie.

- Why do we love disaster movies? Is it because it makes our own lives seem better?

- The very concept of watching movies is bizarre - grown adults listening to fictitious stories. It's childish and yet I do it.

Moving

- If you have too much clutter, force yourself to move. Packing stuff is such a hassle. I find it's easier to just give everything away and start over.

- Packaging items for shipment reminds me of a third grade math problem: "If John seeks the cheapest shipping option, should he ship 16 boxes that are each 1 cubic foot? Or should he ship 1box that's 16 cubic feet?"

- Moving is the ultimate test of friendship. Ask your friends to help you move. Those who help you are true friends. Those who conveniently "can't make it" are not.

- Selling a bed on Craigslist confuses me. I'm never sure if I'm supposed to collect money for selling the bed or pay someone money to remove it?

News

- Most news stations are so negative and sensationalized that there's no point in watching them. I get my news from *The Onion News*. It's just as real and more positive.

- I can predict 50% of the news stories for the next thousand years. There will be "breaking" stories about: shootings, scandals and natural disasters. There's nothing new about it.

Outdoors

- People who go camping aren't actually nature-enthusiasts: they clear cut hiking trails, pollute the Earth with campfires and wear waterproof clothing made from plastic.

- You're more likely to look at the sun if you wear sunglasses. Seems counterproductive.

Parents

- Why do parents pay their kids to do chores? Shouldn't the kids do the chores to pay for room and board?

- As a kid I could never understand why my dad would wear gray socks with jeans, keep a flashlight next to the bed and have day-old coffee cups on his desk. Yet as an adult I absolutely do the same exact things.

Pizza

- True story: I once ordered pizza online and the website required me to create a username and password. I need a password to buy a pizza?

- Are cardboard pizza boxes sanitary? It's not like they're sterilized in a kiln or dishwasher.

- Why are pizzas so massive? It's completely impractical. What other food is served by the square yard?

- Why do we call it a "Margarita" pizza? It tastes nothing like a Margarita.

Phone Calls

- What's the etiquette for calling friends in different time zones? Am I supposed to feel guilty for calling someone at 4 AM? Is it my job to geo-track my friends? Isn't that the very reason why phones have the silence function?

- If I eavesdropped on someone's call while they're on the subway, can I begin offering advice? I just want to be helpful.

- Why is it that people suddenly feel important when they're talking on the phone?

Philosophy

- In life, if you don't know where you're going, you can never be lost.

Poker

- As a general life rule, it's good to surround yourself with winners, except when you're playing poker.

- There are too many fancy combinations in Poker. Rather than saying, "I have a flush," why not say, "I have a lot of cards that look similar" or "I've got some in numeric order"?

- Why do people use chips in poker? The values can easily be changed. A green chip could be worth $1.27 or it could be worth fourteen black chips. Why not use cash?

- Why do poker players tap the table? Seems like a game of *Knock, Knock*.

- Why is it that Poker is the game of choice for mobsters? It seems as arbitrary as playing tennis or basketball.

- If you must make a bet with a friend, make a bet on who will pay for the next vacation. Win or lose, you'll still be happy.

Plants are dangerous because…

- They can be made into spears

- They can fall on you

- You can fall on them

- Roots destroy foundations

- They harbor dangerous wild animals

- They are a leading source of wildfires

Police

- If I'm going to get a speeding ticket, then I'd like some value in return. Maybe a *Thank You* card? Or a free pen? I don't know if the police realize this, but I can take my business to other jurisdictions. Speeding tickets should at least include a hand written *Thank you* note. Then I might be more inclined to leave a tip.

- Nowadays, when a person gets arrested, rather than exercise the right to place one phone call, can he or she make one social media status update?

- I think it's untruthful for an officer to accuse me of speeding seventy miles per hour, when at our latitude, the world is already spinning 700 miles per hour.

- Why do police cars have sirens, brightly flashing lights and the word *Police* written on the sides of the car? They couldn't possibly give criminals any more warning. You don't see the bad guys driving trucks labeled *Robbers*.

Politics

- When voting in an election it's always best to vote for the losing candidate. This way when the winning candidate lets people down, I can explain that it's not my fault.

- Why do people complain when politicians pander? Isn't the job of a politician to please his or her constituents?

- Politicians find it's easier to rewrite the past rather than changing the present.

- How is "donating" to a campaign any different than bribing it?

- What on Earth are donors thinking when they sign up for political fundraisers? "Honey, let's get dressed up this Friday night and talk about taxes."

- Given that politicians are such terrible people, why are their roles considered prestigious?

- I know I can't *buy* a person's vote, but can I pay them to not vote?

- Why do we waste an entire year on US Presidential elections? The President is in office for four years and 25% of his or her time is wasted campaigning.

- Ever watch a political debate? The responses are such convoluted malarkey that I can never recall the original question.

- Voting for politicians is disheartening. It's like being asked, "Do you want to be kicked in the nose or punched in the nose?" There's no good solution.

- Nationwide, liberals tend to live in urban areas while conservatives tend to live in rural areas. The two groups hate each other so much, why don't we just make all the cities one country, and all the rural areas a different country?

- Why do voters listen to political endorsements by Hollywood actors? Don't voters realize that actors lie as a profession?

Random Thoughts

- Why do people say, "No pun intended?" The pun is always intended. Stop lying.

- Why do candles come in delicious scents like *Raspberry Creme Brûlée*? It only tempts me to eat them.

- I don't like crosswalks with the icon of a walking person. It seems like a passive aggressive way to deter me from running or skipping.

Real Estate

- The *Dead-End* street should be rebranded; it's so negative. Call it the "Starting-line street."

- True story: In Boston there's a street named *Dummer Street.* Who would want to live there? And yet, a major university has its campus there.

Relationships

- Why do men give women flowers? "I killed this weak plant to impress you." How is that romantic?

- I could take my girlfriend to a five-star restaurant to celebrate our anniversary, but I prefer to cook at home. How can any food produced by a business have the same sentimental meaning as a homemade dinner? I'm not cheap, I'm sentimental.

- If money doesn't affect love then why do married people combine assets?

- If a woman stands me up for a dinner date, it means I can rationalize spending twice as much on my meal. I love it when women cancel dates.

- One hundred percent of people who get divorced were previously married. Indisputably, marriage is the leading cause of divorce.

Restaurants

- I love restaurant menus where the price is advertised as "market price." It's brilliant. They can charge any price they wish.

- If I'm eating barbecued ribs at a fancy restaurant, must I use a fork and knife?

- Why do they have menus at restaurants? I just want the very best food. They should just list two menu items: 1) The Best Food 2) The Worst Food.

- When I don't want one of the ingredients on my meal at a restaurant, I tell them I'm allergic. Otherwise they disregard my request.

- I like to order at restaurants without using the menu. It makes me feel important.

- Why are meal times so rigid? Why are we supposed to eat just three times per day? In the wild, do sharks only eat during designated breakfast, lunch and dinner times?

- Why does dinner always cost five times more than breakfast? You're eating a meal. A meal is a meal. Cost should be consistent.

Roommates

- If your roommates ever complain that your music is playing too loudly, tell them it's impolite to eavesdrop.

- If you want a good passive aggressive way to get back at your roommate, use all the hot water while he or she is taking a shower. Turn on the dishwasher, turn on the clothes washer and run the kitchen sink at full blast.

Shopping

- I love tracking packages when I order online. It makes me feel important when people report to me.

- I love electronic cash registers in stores because I can feed them ugly dollar bills. Normally a human cashier would give me a hard time.

- Why is the day after Thanksgiving called Black Friday? Isn't Black Monday the day the stock market crashed in 1987?

- Why don't stores have price tags anymore? Is it so unreasonable that I want to know the cost of goods before I buy them? I have no shame in asking for the cost of a product before I buy it.

- I find that returning stuff is more satisfying than buying it. I love getting paid to leave a store.

Society

- Where do people get the nerve to demand to be reminded of something? Has someone ever said to you, "Remind me to (insert name of chore)"? Do they think you are their personal assistant?

- Why do people ever give looks? Why don't they just speak their mind? Looks are more difficult to interpret than words.

- Why do people listen more closely to attractive spokesmodels? Do their looks have anything to do with their intelligence?

- Why is there a stereotype of starving artists? Rockstars are artists, and they're often millionaires.

- Purses seem like a poor design. Why do women flaunt the exact location where they carry their money? It just seems like an invitation to get robbed.

- It's okay to follow irrational and mindless activities. It's called following tradition.

Sports

- Why do people watch sports live? Can't they save time and read the results later?

- I'm not saying football players are wimps but why the helmets and shoulder pads? I thought they were supposed to be tough?

- I find it deceiving when people claim their team won a game. Unless they own stock in the team or played on the team, there is no real ownership.

- If I'm wearing a reflective vest while running, doesn't that make me a target for reckless drivers? I feel safer wearing black while running at night.

- If jocks are so smart then why do they need their names printed on their shirts?

Subway

- I love the subway. I feel like I'm in *Mario Brothers* and I'm taking the warp zone. The darkness of the tunnels feels like traveling through space. I tell myself these things to make an otherwise mundane trip exciting.

- Subways are magnets for crazy people in the most bizarre outfits. If you ever think you're crazy, just compare yourself to people in the subway and you'll feel normal.

Tipping

- Am I allowed to tip the TSA at the airport?

- I believe hazardous workplace conditions justify more tipping. Serving hot coffee, quickly delivering a pizza and cooking with fire all have their fair share of risk.

- As a rule, the tip can only be paid after the food service has been provided. I dislike counter service where they expect a tip before I've received my food. It seems presumptuous. How do I know how much to tip when I don't know how the food tastes or if the service is good?

- Waiters and waitresses usually give me a bad look when I order the cheapest menu item. But in actuality they should be thrilled; by saving money on the food, I have more money that I can use on the tip.

- Why am I expected to tip at the coffee shop but not at the auto mechanic or dentist? Seems rude.

Technology

- We can fly to the moon and harness nuclear energy. Yet our best scientific theory for how the world was created is called the "Big Bang Theory." It sounds like a story made up by a third-grader.

- Why do I have four remote controls to operate my home entertainment system? And how is it that I have a ten gallon bin full of cables and adaptors? I thought that technology is supposed to make our lives easier.

- I always see these warnings: "This website uses cookies. Do you accept?" As if I have a choice? As if I even know what they're tracking?

- True story: My 5-year-old nephew found an old Lego piece of a traditional phone. He asked me what it was. I tried explaining how old phones didn't have touch screens. He thought I was crazy.

- I hate those security questions that are required to verify my identity. I feel like they're too invasive. The security question might be: "What's your favorite color?" I'll enter something random like *bison* just to throw them off. But then a month later I'll be unable to reset my password, so I just stop using the account.

- As a rule, text messages should not exceed three lines. Beyond that, it is inefficient and people should speak by phone.

- I can never figure out how to reset my watch for daylight savings. So I have one watch for the fall and one watch for the spring.

- When I use Google maps, I feel like a spy using a satellite on a secret mission. It makes me feel important.

- Why does the hour have sixty minutes? Who were the numskulls who invented the system of time? If I ruled the world, there would be ten seconds to a minute, ten minutes to an hour and ten hours to the day.

- True story: My electric company required that I create a very complex password to access my account. I then told my electric company that I'm not worried about hackers paying my electric bill.

- How is it these multi-billion-dollar tech companies are run by brilliant people, yet their companies have the most ridiculous names. It's as if they choose a bunch of random letters and jam them together. Yahoo, Hulu, Uber and Google? Yet, somehow these are real companies.

- If I'm unable to pass a Captcha password test does that mean I'm not human?

- Do women respect men who use emojis to converse while texting?

- I'm glad I receive several spam emails per day. Deleting them gives me a sense of accomplishment and makes me feel important.

- I like listening to YouTube videos accelerated at twice the original speed. It makes me feel smarter. After watching hundreds of videos, people in real life sound slow.

- Have you ever been so frustrated at your computer that you wanted to smash it? Why is it we feel that hitting or smashing a computer will motivate it?

- I would like to propose a name to Apple's newest tech gadget. The name will be the "iDontCare."

Terrible Expressions

- I despise the expression: "That's like comparing apples and oranges." The expression is intended to denote two very different items, yet in reality they're both spherical pieces of fruit. I'm lobbying for a new more effective expression: "That's like comparing apples and granite blocks."

- Why do we use the phrase *cold blooded* to describe mean people? Fish are cold blooded and they never hurt people. In fact, fish help feed people. Being labeled *cold blooded* should be a compliment.

Weather

- Why are meteorologists so negative? Why do they say, "It'll be partly cloudy" when they could say, "There will be light sun today"?

- Rather than saying, "There's a ten percent chance of rain," why don't they just admit, "We're just guessing today"?

- Umbrellas are good passive aggressive weapons. I sometimes use them to dump water on rude people.

- The choice of whether to use an umbrella or raincoat is as debatable an issue as religion.

Weddings

- Diamond rings are a scam. Your true friends shouldn't care if it's real and everyone else can't tell anyway. So why bother getting a real one?

- Spending money on a lavish wedding is like spending money on college. Once people do it, they don't want to admit the financial mistake.

Work

- On my resume I wrote that "I have excellent luck," because I consider it a key skill.

About The Author

Matt Byron AKA "Byron" has also written:

Byron's Prepper Humor and Survival Guide
How to Conquer a Nation
The Art of Spin
Live Your Dreams

Byron's other books and YouTube comedy series can be found at: MattByron.com

If you enjoyed this book, please recommend it to your friends or write a review on Amazon.com. If you disliked this book, please recommend it to your greatest nemesis. Thank you!